THE MOVIE

A CHORUS LINE

mpL

Published by
MPL COMMUNICATIONS, INC.

Exclusively distributed by
HAL LEONARD PUBLISHING CORPORATION
Winona, MN 55987   Milwaukee, WI 53213

ISBN 0-88188-434-0

CONTENTS

Music by MARVIN HAMLISCH
Lyrics by EDWARD KLEBAN

Applications for performance of this work, whether legitimate, stock,
amateur, or foreign, should be addressed to:
TAMS-WITMARK
560 Lexington Avenue
New York, N.Y., 10022

Decision time and just sixteen dancers, eight girls and eight boys, are selected from the morning's hundreds. Assistant choreographer, Larry **TERRENCE MANN,** lines up dancers, (left to right) Don **BLANE SAVAGE,** Maggie **PAM KLINGER,** Mike **CHARLES McGOWAN,** Connie **JAN GAN BOYD,** Greg **JUSTIN ROSS,** Sheila **VICKI FREDERICK,** Bobby **MATT WEST,** Bebe **MICHELLE JOHNSTON,** Judy **JANET JONES,** Richie **GREGG BURGE,** Al **TONY FIELDS,** Kristine **NICOLE FOSSE,** Val **AUDREY LANDERS,** Mark **MICHAEL BLEVINS,** Paul **CAMERON ENGLISH,** and Morales **YAMIL BORGES** in Sir Richard Attenborough's "A CHORUS LINE" from Embassy Films Associates in association with Polygram Pictures.

I HOPE I GET IT

Music by MARVIN HAMLISCH
Lyric by EDWARD KLEBAN

Please God, I need this job. I've got to get this job.

(Zach:) O.K. First group, ballet combination. Everybody else clear the

stage. Second group, be ready.

1 - 2 - 3 - 4 - 5 - 6

Boy solo: God, I real-ly blew it! I real-ly blew it.

Girl solo: How could I do a thing like

WHO AM I ANYWAY?

Music by MARVIN HAMLISCH
Lyric by EDWARD KLEBAN

I Can Do That

Music by MARVIN HAMLISCH
Lyric by EDWARD KLEBAN

AT THE BALLET

Music by MARVIN HAMLISCH
Lyric by EDWARD KLEBAN

Intense, emotional, driving

Dad-dy al-ways thought that he mar-ried be-neath him. That's what he said, that's what he said. When he pro-posed he in-formed my moth-er he was prob-ab-ly her ver-y last chance. And

28

29

32

ev - 'ry - thing __ was beau - ti - ful __ at the bal - let, _____ at the

bal - let, _____ at the bal - let!!! _____

Yes,

SURPRISE, SURPRISE

Music by MARVIN HAMLISCH
Lyric by EDWARD KLEBAN

OPENING — The Company

"WHO AM I ANYWAY?" — Cameron English (Paul)

"I CAN DO THAT" — Charles McGowan (Mike)

"HELLO TWELVE" — The Company

"SURPRISE, SURPRISE" — Gregg Burge (Richie)
Chorus by The Company

"NOTHING" — Yamil Borges (Morales)

"DANCE: TEN; LOOKS: THREE" — Audrey Landers (Val)

"LET ME DANCE FOR YOU" — Alyson Reed (Cassie)

"DANCE: TEN; LOOKS: THREE" — Audrey Landers (Val)

"WHAT I DID FOR LOVE" — Alyson Reed (Cassie)

"ONE" — The Company

HELLO TWELVE, HELLO THIRTEEN, HELLO LOVE

Music by MARVIN HAMLISCH
Lyric by EDWARD KLEBAN

NOTHING

Music by MARVIN HAMLISCH
Lyric by EDWARD KLEBAN

I'm so excited because I'm gonna go to the High School of Performing Arts.
I mean, I was dying to be a serious actress. Anyway it's the first day
of acting class and we're in the auditorium and the teacher, Mister Karp,
puts us up on the stage with our legs around everybody, one in back of
the other, and he says: O.K., we're gonna do improvisations. Now, you're
on a bobsled and it's snowing out and it's cold. O. K., go!

Light Rock *(Repeat as needed under spoken introduction)*

Ev - 'ry-day   for a   week we would try to   feel   the   mo - tion,
Sec - ond week,   more ad - vanced and we   had to   be   a   ta - ble,

feel   the   mo - tion   down the hill. _____
be   a   sports car...   ice cream cone. _____

52

I'm feel - ing noth-ing," _____ and he says, "Noth -ing could

get a girl trans - fered." They all felt some - thing, ___

but I felt noth - ing _____ ex - cept the feel - ing that this

bull - shit was ab - surd! *But I said to myself, "Hey! it's*

54

LET ME DANCE FOR YOU

Music by MARVIN HAMLISCH
Lyric by EDWARD KLEBAN

63

DANCE: TEN; LOOKS: THREE

Music by MARVIN HAMLISCH
Lyric by EDWARD KLEBAN

ONE

Music by MARVIN HAMLISCH
Lyric by EDWARD KLEBAN

Moderately

One sin - gu - lar sen - sa - tion ev - 'ry lit - tle step she takes.

One thrill - ing com - bi - na - tion ev - 'ry move that she makes.

One smile and sud - den - ly no - bod - y

Repeat and fade

WHAT I DID FOR LOVE

Music by MARVIN HAMLISCH
Lyric by EDWARD KLEBAN

82

AT THE BALLET

Music by MARVIN HAMLISCH
Lyric by EDWARD KLEBAN

Daddy always thought that he married beneath him,
That's what he said, that's what he said.
When he proposed he informed my mother
He was probably her very last chance.
And though she was twenty-two, though she was
    twenty-two,
Though she was twenty-two, she married him.
Life with my dad wasn't ever a picnic,
More like a "Come as you are."
When I was five I remember my mother
Dug earrings out of the car.
I knew they weren't hers, but it wasn't something
You'd wanna discuss.
He wasn't warm, *well, not to her. . . well, not to us!*
But ev'rything was beautiful at the ballet,
Graceful men lift lovely girls in white.
Yes, ev'rything was beautiful at the ballet,
Hey! I was happy at the ballet.
Up a steep and very narrow stairway to the voice
    like a metronome.
Up a steep and very narrow stairway, it wasn't Paradise,
It wasn't Paradise, it wasn't Paradise, but it was home.
Mother always said I'd be very attractive
When I grew up, when I grew up.
"Diff'rent", she said, "With a special something
And a very, very personal flair."
And though I was eight or nine, though I was eight or nine,
Though I was eight or nine, I hated her.
Now "diff'rent" is nice, but it sure isn't pretty.
"Pretty" is what it's about.
I never met anyone who was "diff'rent"
Who couldn't figure that out.
So beautiful I'd never live to see
But it was clear, *if not to her, well, then to me!*
That ev'ryone is beautiful at the ballet.
Ev'ry prince has got to have his swan.
Yes, ev'ryone is beautiful at the ballet.
Hey! I was pretty at the ballet.
Up a steep and very narrow stairway to the voice
    like a metronome.
Up a steep and very narrow stairway, it wasn't Paradise,
It wasn't Paradise, it wasn't Paradise, but it was home.
Ev'rything was beautiful at the ballet.
Raise your arms and someone's always there.
Yes, ev'rything was beautiful at the ballet,
Hey! I was pretty, I was happy,
"I would love to". . . At the ballet.

DANCE: TEN; LOOKS: THREE

Music by MARVIN HAMLISCH
Lyric by EDWARD KLEBAN

Dance: Ten; Looks: Three
And I'm still on unemployment,
Dancing for my own enjoyment.
That ain't it, kid! That ain't it, kid!
Dance: Ten; Looks: Three is like to die.
Left the the'ter and called the doctor
For my appointment to buy. . .
Tits and ass. Bought myself a fancy pair.
Tightened up the derriere.
Did the nose with it, all that goes with it.
Tits and ass! Had the bingo-bongos done.
Suddenly I'm getting Nash'nal tours!
Tits and ass won't get you jobs,
Unless they're yours.
Didn't cost a fortune, neither.
Didn't hurt my sex life, either.
Flat and sassy, I would get the strays and losers,
Beggars really can't be choosers.
That ain't it, kid! That ain't it, kid!

Fixed the chassis, "How do you do!"
Life turned into an endless medley of
"Gee, it had to be you." *Why?*
Tits and ass. Where the cupboard once was bare,
Now you knock and someone's there.
You have got 'em, hey! Top to bottom, hey!
It's a gas! Just a dash of silicone.
Shake your new maracas and you're fine!
Tits and ass can change your life,
They sure changed mine.
Have it all done. Honey, take my word.
Grab a cab, c'mon, see the wizard on Park and
    Seventy Third
For tits and ass. Orchestra and balcony.
What they want is what cha see.
Keep the best of you, do the rest of you.
Pits or class, I have never seen it fail,
Debutante or chorus girl or wife.
Tits and ass, yes, tits and ass have changed my life.

HELLO TWELVE, HELLO THIRTEEN, HELLO LOVE

Music by MARVIN HAMLISCH
Lyric by EDWARD KLEBAN

Hello Twelve, Hello Thirteen, Hello Love.
Changes, Oh! down below, up above.
Time to doubt, to break out, it's a mess.
(It's a mess.)
Time to grow, time to go adolesce.
(Adolesce.)
Too young to take over, too old to ignore.
Gee, I'm almost ready, *but what for?*
There's a lot I am not certain of.
Hello Twelve, Hello Thirteen, Hello Love.

I CAN DO THAT

Music by MARVIN HAMLISCH
Lyric by EDWARD KLEBAN

I'm watchin' Sis go pit-a-pat,
Said, I can do that, I can do that.
Knew ev'ry step right off the bat,
Said, I can do that, I can do that.
One morning Sis won't go to dance class,
I grab her shoes and tights and all,
But my foot's too small, so,
I stuff her shoes with extra socks,
Run seven blocks in nothin' flat,
Hell, I can do that, I can do that.
I got to class and had it made,
And so I stayed the rest of my life.
All thanks to Sis, (now married and fat)
I can do this.
That I can do, I can do that.

I HOPE I GET IT

Music by MARVIN HAMLISCH
Lyric by EDWARD KLEBAN

(Zach:) Again! Step, kick, kick, leap, kick, touch.
Again! Step, kick, kick, leap, kick, touch.
Again! Step, kick, kick, leap, kick, touch.
Again! Step, kick, kick, leap, kick, touch.
Right! That connects with turn, turn out, in touch, step,
Step, kick, kick, leap, kick, touch.
Got it? Going on and turn, turn, touch down,
Back step, pivot step, walk, walk, walk. Right!
Let's do the whole combination facing away from the mirror.
From the top! 5, 6, 7, 8!
(All:) God, I hope I get it, I hope I get it.
How many people does he need?
(Boys:) How many people does he need?
(All:) God, I Hope I get it. I hope I get it.
How many boys, how many
(Boys:) girls?
(Girls:) How many boys, how many..?
(Boys:) Look at all the people!...At all the people.
How many people does he need?
How many boys? How many girls?
How many people does he...?
(Solo:) I really need this job.
Please, God, I need this job.
I've got to get this job!
(Zach:) Stage left, boys.
Let's do the ballet combination,
First group of girls, second group to follow.
1, 2, 3, 4, 5, 6.
(All:) God, I really blew it! I really blew it.
How could I do a thing like that?
How could I do a thing like...?
Now, I'll never make it; I'll never make it!
He doesn't like the way I look.
He doesn't like the way I dance.
He doesn't like the way I...
(Zach:) Alright, let me see the boys.
The whole group. Ready, 5, 6, 7, 8!
Okay, Girls, 5, 6, 7, 8!
(Group:) God, I think I've got it.
I think I've got it. I knew he liked me all the time.
Still, it isn't over. It isn't over.
I can't imagine what he wants. I can't imagine what he...
God, I hope I get it! I hope I get it.
I've come this far, but even so:
It could be yes, it could be no.
How many people does he..?
(Others:) I really need this job.
Please, God, I need this job.
(All:) I've got to get this show.
(Paul:) Who am I anyway? Am I my resume?
That is a picture of a person I don't know.
What does he want from me?
What should I try to be?
So many faces all around, and here we go.
I need this job. Oh God, I need this show.

LET ME DANCE FOR YOU

Music by MARVIN HAMLISCH
Lyric by EDWARD KLEBAN

I am a dancer.
That's who I am, what I do.
I. . .I am a dancer.
Give me the steps, I'll come through.
Give me somebody to dance for, give me somebody
  to show.
Let me wake up in the morning to find I have somewhere
  exciting to go.

Let me dance for you, let me try.
Let me dance for you.
We made a lot of music dancing, you and I.

Please, give me an answer, give me a place to begin.
I. . .I am a dancer.
I have come home, let me in.
Give me somebody to dance with, give me somebody
  to be.
Let me wake up feeling terribly proud that the girl in the
  mirror is me.

Let me dance for you, let me try.
Let me dance for you.
We made a lot of music dancing, you and I.
Let me dance for you, let me try.
Let me dance for you.
We made a lot of lovely music dancing.
Let me dance for you, let me try.
Let me dance for you.
We made a lot of music dancing you and I.

NOTHING

Music by MARVIN HAMLISCH
Lyric by EDWARD KLEBAN

Ev'ryday for a week we would try to feel the motion,
Feel the motion down the hill.
Ev'ryday day for a week we would try to hear the wind rush,
Hear the wind rush, feel the chill.
And I dug right down to the bottom of my soul to see
What I had inside.
Yes, I dug right down to the bottom of my soul and I tried,
I tried.
And everybody's going Woosh. . . .woosh. . . . . .
I feel the snow, I feel the cold. . .I feel the air.''
And Mr. Karp turns to me and he says,
"O.K., Morales, what did you feel?"
And I said, "Nothing, I'm feeling nothing."
And he says, "Nothing could get a girl transfered."
They all felt something, but I felt nothing
Except the feeling that this bull-shit was absurd!
But, I said to myself, "Hey! it's only the first week.
Maybe it's genetic, they don't have bobsleds in
  San Juan!"
Second week, more advanced and we had to be a table,
Be a sports car. . .ice cream cone.
Mister Karp, he would say, "Very good, except Morales.
Try, Morales, all alone."
So I dug right down to the bottom of my soul to see
How an ice cream felt.
Yes, I dug right down to the bottom of my soul and I tried
To melt.

The kids yelled "Nothing!" They called me "Nothing"
And Karp allowed it, which really makes me burn.
They were so helpful, they called me "Hopeless",
Until I really didn't know where else to turn.
And Karp kept saying,
"Morales, I think you should transfer to Girl's High. . .
You'll never be an actress. Never!" Jesus Christ!
Went to church, praying, Santa Maria, send me guidance,
Send me guidance on my knees.
Went to church, praying, Santa Maria, help me feel it,
Help me feel it, pretty please.
And a voice from down at the bottom of my soul came up
To the top of my head,
And the voice from down at the bottom of my soul,
Here is what it said:
This man is nothing, this course is nothing,
If you want something, go find another class.
And when you find one you'll be an actress.
And I assure you that's what fin'lly came to pass.
Six months later I heard that Karp had died.
And I dug right down to the bottom of my soul. . .and cried
'Cause I felt nothing.

ONE

Music by MARVIN HAMLISCH
Lyric by EDWARD KLEBAN

One singular sensation ev'ry little step she takes.
One thrilling combination ev'ry move that she makes.
One smile and suddenly nobody else will do
You know you'll never be lonely with you-know-who.
One moment in her presence and you can forget the rest,
For the girl is second best to none, son.
Ooooh! Sigh! Give her your attention.
Do I really have to mention, she's the one?
She walks into a room and you know
She's uncommonly rare, very unique, peripatetic,
Poetic and chic.
She walks into a room and you know
From her maddening poise, effortless whirl,
She's the special girl strolling,
Can't help all of her qualities extolling.
Loaded with charisma is ma jauntily,
Sauntering, ambling, shambler.
She walks into a room and you know
You must shuffle along, join the parade.
She's the quintessence of making the grade.
This is whatcha call trav'lling!
Oh, strut your stuff. Can't get enough of her.
Love her. I'm a son of a gun, she is one of a kind.
One singular sensation ev'ry little step she takes.
One thrilling combination ev'ry move that she makes.
One smile and suddenly nobody else will do.
You know you'll never be lonely with you-know-who.
One moment in her presence and you can forget the rest,
For the girl is second best to none, son.
Ooooh! Sigh! Give her your attention.
Do I really have to mention, she's the one?

SURPRISE, SURPRISE

Music by MARVIN HAMLISCH
Lyric by EDWARD KLEBAN

First time we made love, it was a great big deal.
I was too scared to feel, nervous from trying.
Next time we made love, still we were not a hit.
I thought, if this is it ev'ryone's lying.
But then we did it again, and I forgot to be scared
I guess; 'cause when we did it again, I closed my eyes:

Surprise, surprise.
Surprise, surprise.
Surprise, surprise.
Surprise!

Sweet, icicle hot, smooth as a lemon pie, sailing across
the sky into the ocean.
We liked it a lot, you can imagine why.
We had begun to fly, feelings in motion.
And then we did it again;
I'm thinking, was it beginner's luck?
Or is it wonderful once in each three tries.

Surprise, surprise.
Surprise, surprise.
Surprise, surprise.
Surprise, surprise.
Surprise, Surprise!

WHAT I DID FOR LOVE

Music by MARVIN HAMLISCH
Lyric by EDWARD KLEBAN

Kiss today good-bye,
The sweetness and the sorrow.
We did what we had to do,
And I can't regret
What I did for love;
What I did for love.
Look, my eyes are dry,
The gift was ours to borrow.
It's as if we always knew,
But I won't forget what I did for love;
What I did for love.
Gone, love is never gone,
As we travel on,
Love's what we'll remember.
Kiss today good-bye,
And point me t'ward tomorrow.
Wish me luck; the same to you.
Won't forget, can't regret
What I did for love.
What I did for love.
What I did for love.

WHO AM I ANYWAY?

Music by MARVIN HAMLISCH
Lyric by EDWARD KLEBAN

Who am I anyway?
Am I my résumé?
That is a picture of a person I don't know.
What does he want from me?
What should I try to be?
So many faces all around, and here we go.
I need this job.
Oh God, I need this show.